Twenty-Four Heartbeats

Tuned by waves of emotion

VAANI GOWDA

BookLeaf Publishing

India | USA | UK

Made with ❤ on the BookLeaf Publishing Platform
www.bookleafpub.in
www.bookleafpub.com

Dedication

To God, the giver of words and wisdom.

To my parents and family- who have always been my backbone.

To beautiful souls who appreciated and encouraged me from the very beginning of this journey- your words built the foundation of who I've become.

Preface

I've written this book to lift every soul clouded by doubt, and to offer a glimpse into the raw reality of life- one often hidden behind noise and illusion. For those who are searching for answers, for hope, or simply a quite space to feel - I offer you my words.

Twenty four Heartbeats means Twenty four hours in a day. Each beat marks a moment in time, the rhythm that drives our lives forward. Each beat is a reflection of my journey- lessons learned, wounds healed, and moments that shaped me into who I am today. I hope they offer you the same comfort, courage and light. Even if one soul finds comfort in these pages, then every word has found it's home.

May this book help you take a deep dive into waves of reality, tune your Heartbeats into a rhythm that feels calmer, softer and more at ease that further helps you treat other's murmurs with kindness and peace.

Acknowledgements

I express my heartfelt gratitude -
To the divine light that guide my every verse.
To my parents and family- my unwavering pillars of strength and support.
To all the well wishers who appreciated my work, nurtured my confidence and inspired me to keep going.
And to those who broke my heart, doubted my worth and tried to dim my light - thank you for unknowingly help me rise, ignite the fire within and shape a better version of myself.

1. Calming one's murmurs

People often try to dim your light,
When they know they can't win the fight,
And that you are capable of climbing to a height.

Their murmurs adds turbulence into your heart,
Making it a disturbed piece of art.

Their heart speaks with jealously,
Making your mind messy,
Hindering your tendency.

Well that's their only way to win,
But ask yourself,
Are you ready to let your colors dry before they can
paint your life?

Let the fire within,
Burn away their noise to coal.
Soundproof your soul.
If peace don't stay, migrate.

Don't let anything blame your fate,
Work hard and watch the light open your gate.

VAANI GOWDA

2. Rhythm of Recovery

The body heals it's wound with time,
so why does the soul linger in pain, even after the hurt
left no stain?

Time heals everything,
The pain and the bleeding,
Yet the scars remain.
Listen to them, don't complain.
They tell stories, that help you gain -Values, ethics and
life lessons.

Rugged path that helps you grow,
Broken bonds tell you where not to go.

Don't be sad because it happened,
Be proud, because you survived.

Healing is non uniform,
Sometimes it repairs, sometimes it injures,
But avoid additional fractures, and stay secure.

VAANI GOWDA

3. Navigating the soul

A mind full of chaos,
Makes a strongest boat sink.

And in a life without compass,
even a calm mind can lead you south instead of east in a
blink.

The water ahead is endless,
Hurdled with gentle and roaring currents.

From rivers to lakes to wide oceans- the journey is
infinite,
sailing with dreams too vast to limit.
But make sure that you live it legit.

Treat everyone with empathy.
Look around and embrace the beauty,
Smile wide and treat everyone gently,
Laugh out loud and let the soul dance swiftly,
Move with ease and breathe quietly,

Let every minute of journey help you shine brightly.

Every journey meets it's end.
What you carry is how you spend.

VAANI GOWDA

4. Loop of Life

From rivers to lakes, to oceans and shores,
Life is a loop.
With all your heart, take your scoop.

The shore is where your new life starts,
Life is a cycle - carry that in your heart.

Dreams, relationships and achievements are just a part,
What truly matters is kindness, peace and moments that
paint the art.

The shore is where the new life starts,
Our past journey maps our cart.

Good deeds drives us to various heights,
Be it in values, knowledge or attainments.

From cart to boat- the cycle is infinite,
We are puppets under divine light,

Bound by fate, that we didn't write.

Life is a cycle -carry that in your heart,
Don't let your ego and evil mind play the dart.

VAANI GOWDA

5. From Sun to Moon- The Journey to Rise and Shine

Life is like a sky,
Set your goals high.
Fasten your tie,
And bid all your distractions a goodbye.

Shine as bright as sun
Imagine the amount of fuel one needs in order to run.
Have hope and faith until you're done.
It might take thirty-one or fourty-one or fifty-one.

Finally one day you glow,
Just like the moon.
With calmness and ease, you bloom.
Wrapped in a cocoon,
At peace with the monsoon.

VAANI GOWDA

6. Toxic hues - Unfiltered Friendships

In a world where women have to stand tall together,
they pull each other down making people walk on one
another.

She offers her hand to help you ascend,
But with clawed hands that leave you drained.
Jealousy disguised as care,
Leaving your confidence stripped bare.
Pretends to be supportive,
And in reality, her words are emotionally assaultive.

She loves to play a real friend card,
Only when others are around.
She shares only your reaction, but never the actions that
provoked it.

Her words are indirect,
But her aim is always perfect.
She makes you feel anxious and insecure,

With a mindset that she's superior.
Turns connection into competition,
Slowly ruining your ethics and ambition.

In the name of friendship, never entertain toxicity,
And ruin your authenticity.
Cut them off, or you will watch them play off.

VAANI GOWDA

7. Heartbeats in Harmony

A smile so vivid,
Knitted with colors so lucid.

The voice that keeps echoing,
Midst the cows that keep mooing.

Eyes filled with love so eternal,
Indulged in honey that makes it surreal.

Words chained with pearls of trust and respect.
One's presence that makes life perfect.

The moments that toil so deep in heart,
Forming a string that nothing can break apart.

VAANI GOWDA

8. Fleeting Heartbeats

How can symbol of heart have only a single bend?
Isn't it made for two souls to blend?

The true love watered it's growing plant,
While the shallow love forgot to show it's spark.

The deep love gave all it's part,
But the shallow love had a stony heart.

How can one clap with single hand?
Life is too short to let our energy get drained!

How can one paint a beautiful art with a faded colors?
Life isn't perfect without contrast colors!
Art is made to be vibrant and full of life.
Not something that brings tears in your eyes.

VAANI GOWDA

9. Strength in Softness

Let us try to be kind,
Even in the darkest grooves of our mind,
Keeping the ego and the anger behind.

Let the warmth within you melt the ice,
Because being hard is only gonna add spice.

VAANI GOWDA

10. Gentle waves - That tune the soul

A ray of light,
Amidst the deadly night.
Offers her shoulder to lean on,
When the world plays a con.

In the world where women is women's worst enemy,
She proves that not all are frenemies.
In the world where women compete,
Her support and kindness hit you deep.

She is a light that keeps your belief in friendship
glowing,
And waters the plant that keeps on growing.

She sees your sorrows as if they were her own,
And never allows you linger in them alone.

As soon as you walk inside a classroom,
Her presence makes you bloom.

There is comfort in her words,
That feels like a chirping of birds.

VAANI GOWDA

11. Waves of emotions

Tears are meant to be shed off,
Holding back only tears you off.

It's not a symbol of weakness,
But a sign of strength and wholeness.

A silent healing in disguise,
That shows up as pearls that roll down gently,
And leaves behind a glow that fires quietly.

Emotions are not meant to be suppressed,
But to be acknowledged.

People without empathy,
Often say it's for gaining sympathy.

They are more like a scarecrow,
Emotionless and heart stuffed with straw.

Being emotional isn't a flaw,
It's a sign that you are unfiltered and raw.

VAANI GOWDA

12. Love Beyond Boundaries

How can a bird and a fish fall in love?

How can they?
Will the sky and the sea keep them away?
Love isn't about where you belong,
But whether, it will last lifelong..

Must they really be alike?
Must they both live only in air or in water?
Would that not clip their Wings and Fins?
While that had to help them pursue things..

Love should never bring one pain, for how can joy
remain if the other is chained?

Love doesn't last in being the same,
but walking together even in the rain.
It's one's choice to hold an umbrella or let their love fade
in the rain.

Wings and Fins, a love beyond boundaries.
On the horizon, creating memories...

VAANI GOWDA

13. The Truth Beneath

Everyone's life seems to move in perfect rhythm,
Filled with light, harmony and grace.
Just like a lotus - serene and flawless.

Only when one dives deep,
Is the shallowness truly seen.

The mud and debris that leaves it's stain,
Along with tadpole and fishes that causes pain.

The roots, fewer and shorter,
Makes the foundation like a weak mortar.

The untold stories, so dark,
That bring no spark.

Chilled water disrupts the rhythm,
Instilling chaos among organism.

No one's life is truly perfect,
What you see is all that reflects.

VAANI GOWDA

14. The Power of Wind

A toddler absorbs fresh sight and adventure from their
surrounding,
Just like that our friend circle moulds our upbringing.

Energy flows from highest potential to it's lowest
potential,
Don't you feel it applies to us as well?
If I find my energy getting drained and hard to dwell,
I make sure that I bid you a good farewell.

Hang out with people who help you rise,
The one's who motivate you to aim for skies.

VAANI GOWDA

15. A Subtle Art of Forgiving

Do you know anyone who is perfect?
Someone without a single flaw?
The one who eats even without opening their jaw?

None of our lives are like white flour,
We've all slipped atleast once on a wet floor,
Some people often act based their mood,
Or maybe it's simply how far they have evolved.

Hating or judging a person isn't breezy,
It only makes your own life feel frizzy.

Our life is like an endless sea,
Some are just a branch of tree, maybe just a bee.
To focus on your degree,
Your mind has to be completely free,
Hence forgiveness is the only key.

VAANI GOWDA

16. The Mountains and Milestones

Every mountain has a peak,
We may ascend or descend,
Toiling through tough obstacles,
Teaches you to face the struggles.

After deceleration, you may accelerate,
Perhaps to even greater height.
Stay strong and fight,
Until you shine bright.

Every mountain has a summit,
If you are slipping, perhaps it's not your route.
Reroute without doubt;
with faith, chase your bait,
new opportunities await.

If you don't want to switch your track,
Build your stack, and crack the hack,
Look back and build your hope,

And see how far you've coped.

Along the course,
Don't let the wind, control your force,
Embrace the path you chose,
It's not just the destination, but the journey that grows.

VAANI GOWDA

17. The Hidden Cost of Social Media

A boon to humanity,
Provided you use it with care and humility.

Be mindful about the dose,
Don't let it take away your toast.

One's life is never truly close,
The host only shows the best, at most,
For all they do is boast.

Virtual connection may draw us close,
But they place our true moments at stake, I suppose.

It sparks comparison between people,
Making one fickle, like an eagle.

It does connect us with our surroundings,
But clips away our grounding.

Likes and followers are an illusion,
Often leading you into delusion.

Filters and edits are the culprits,
Dimming your spirit, hiding the true fit.

Virtual validations,
And empty temptations,
Twist your connotation.

It creates obsession,
Diving you into anxiety and depression,
And halts your progression.

Social media is just on phone,
Shut it off and see what you own,
Don't let anything bring you down.

VAANI GOWDA

18. The Silent Struggle

The battle with our emotions,
Amidst the roaring oceans.
Often goes unnoticed,
Like the hands of anesthetist.

Heart submerged in chaos,
Beats tunes of flaws.
Slowly turning you into a grandma,
with signs of aging,
we find ourselves fading.

Gauze the heart, untune the beat,
And turn off the tweets.

The Silent battle with ourselves,
Seeks our help,
But sadly, at times that's not found in our well,
And have no capacity to dwell.

We often find no answer,

But can truly chose a sponsor,
At least that might act as an enhancer.
Making our soul a dancer.

VAANI GOWDA

19. The Rumors

Rumors are like restless wind,
Turns sharp eyes blind.
The wind that winds the gentle breeze,
Moves through the trees and over the seas,
Gathering all the impurities,
Slowly reshaping the realities.

When anyone spills the tea,
It may contain debris,
Hence judge nobody.

People justify a person based on their view,
Which may distort the lens of what's true,
Before judging take time and see,
Gentle breeze and roaring currents make up the sea.

VAANI GOWDA

20. To Conquer

The true success is to conquer your emotions,
Not by suppressing them,
but by acknowledging their motions.
Embrace every waves that rise within,
Learn from the tides, and see where they. guide.

Suffering is a choice, so silence your voice.
Notice the joys, agony only adds spice.
Don't be too cold nor an emotional fool,
Both will drown you deep into same pool.

VAANI GOWDA

21. Men and Their Challeges: Internal or External Battle

U or I can only know that in disguise,
As we can only judge through our eyes,
For not all men walk in same shoes,
Commenting based on one's path, can make it a due.
But, in my opinion, it's more like a bruise
For anything to bleed from inside,
has to be due to a force from outside.

Societal expectations to fear of failure.
Relationship challenges to financial pressure.
Life adds thorns on their way.
Yet they walk masking it away.

VAANI GOWDA

22. A Heavenly Bond

Bonds are made in heaven,
Woven with threads so divine.

Glowing like a sacred shrine,
Hard to unwind.

A bond so strong,
Might melt when the other is wrong,
But still stays strong, enduring long.

A bond beyond words,
Love, care, trust blend like song from keyboard.
Hard to express,
But enough to impress,
And everything else, suppressed.

VAANI GOWDA

23. A Broken Bond

Bonds are made in heaven,
But this one was burned.
Each soul we meet is destined,
Yet this one was removed.

The emotional debt ties us through seven lives,
Maybe this one is free - free of debt,
That had to binds us through lives.

Each fight or a misunderstanding was just a reason.
For the life to drive us towards it's destined vision.

We are puppets under destiny's art,
Tied by threads we can't outsmart.

VAANI GOWDA

24. The Mask of Makeup

You mask your scars and blemishes from the world,
But not from the mirror of your own soul.

People who taunt are soulless,
Hiding their own emptiness behind cruel words.

Make up is a mask that fakes up.
Never get roped into the beauty standards.
You are beautiful- maskless and filterless.

You know how beautiful you are from inside,
Don't give your ears to people outside.

VAANI GOWDA

25. Surroundings Influence Success

A peaceful mind is important,
To reach any distant.
Surrounding chaos and fights,
Crubs you from climbing heights.

A house has to be a home,
Not just sticks scattered by storm,
Nor a hollow carved by worm,
But where each stick is equal - like a teeth of comb.

A comb works efficiently when all it's teeth are equal.
Where nobody is a sequel.

Each teeth plays a part,
If you look deep into the art,
where each stoke acts like a dart.

VAANI GOWDA

26. A Journey Through Railway Stations

Life is like a railway track,
Where each station acts like a stack,
A milestone reached, a battle achieved.

Throughout our journey,
We reach multiple stations,
Each station watches people come and go,
Getting in, moving out, just as in life too.

Greet everyone with love and care,
You never know when their station will arrive.
In a blink of an eye, they might be gone,
Even before the arrival of dawn.

Embrace your path, and stay on track,
It will take you to your destined rack.

VAANI GOWDA

27. Moments of Joy

Moments of joy,
When we played with our favorite toy.

Moments of joy,
After our mother calmed us from our cry.

Moments of bliss,
When we received our first kiss.

Moments of bliss,
After the gain of benefits.

Moments of happiness,
When we gain a bonus.

Moments of cheer,
When they're from our dear and near.

Moments of delight,
When dreams take their flight.

Moments of delight,
When something soothes your sight.

Moments of warmth,
Where love takes every form.

Moments of hope,
When you learnt to cope.

Moments of peace,
Where whole world cease.

Moments of love,
That's actually blessing from above.

These are the moments we live for,
When life feels rich with hearts that explore.

VAANI GOWDA

28. The Fading Colors of Sky

Initially, the sky is purple,
The clouds are soft and pink,
But as the wind blows,
Will those colors cease.

Colors fade, but their essence remain.
Though the sky may lose its hue,
The memory will stay true.

VAANI GOWDA

29. Redefining Age

We often define age by the years we survive,
While it should be by the moments we have truly felt
alive.

Not by the aging of cells,
But by the art painted with pastels.

Not by the time that's running,
But my the milestones achieved and forthcoming.

We age by the happy moments lived,
The Battles survived,
And the goals achieved.

VAANI GOWDA

30. The Summer and Winter

The scorching summer sun reminds us of winter's cool
breeze.
The winters cool breeze reminds us of warmth of sun by
the seas.

The summer wets our cloth,
While the winter spreads our bedcloth

The summer loves the sweat,
And the winter waits for the sunset.

The summer taunts the cool breeze,
While the winter cheers the gentle freeze.

Summer teaches us to endure the heat,
While the winter reminds us how time fleets.
Both seasons pass, teaching us to surpass.
We find strength in change and the paths we embrace.

VAANI GOWDA

31. Faith

Unwavering belief in someone's love and intention,
That grows a deeper connection.

The bond stays strong even during storms of doubt,
Clearing the paths, where new hopes sprout.

People say it isn't something that's earned,
But a strong hope with doubts burned.
But in reality, it earned,
Through the love, care and loyalty that's returned.

VAANI GOWDA

32. Loyalty: The Soul of Connection

A foundation of a meaningful relationship,
Rooted in trust and loving companionship.

A silent promise that brings pure bliss.
Strengthens trust- a win over lust.

It engraves a deeper emotional connection,
Slowly blooming into true affection.

A commitment in love,
like in a faithful dove.

It's the heart of lasting relationship,
That fosters a friendship pure and deep.

Loyalty gives our love true meaning,
Without it, the hearts begins depleting.

VAANI GOWDA

33. The Orphan

The longing for love that's never been seen,
A desire to rest on the lap of a queen.
Hearts filled with hope and prayer,
Waiting for the love to draw them there.

The TV screens that ripen their dream,
A dream that never gets to gleam.

A life shed in poverty,
Where the nurture and care slipped into liberty.

They go blaming their fate,
Asking why the destiny holds so much hate.

The unheard lullabies,
And the unattended night stories,
Makes them sleep in silence.

The emotional trauma that sinks them deep,
Where they find no answer even when they weep.

They seek to belong, to thrive and to be loved,
Not the sympathy that pulls them down.
For it waters their pain that's already sown.

They learn to battle loneliness,
And stay still in emptiness.
Shaped by fear and insecurity,
They grow too soon into maturity.

VAANI GOWDA

34. Eyes That Live On

Waning abilities due to abnormality,
Let the blind too see the beauty.

Donate your eye,
Don't let it die.
We are gifted,
While some are blind sighted.

An act of charity,
Brings a change in one's functionality,
And blessings from the Lord Almighty.

VAANI GOWDA

35. First Love

A special love, unexplainable in words.
Every moment feels new, like the songs never heard.

What makes it so special?
Is it that it's untouched by experiences?
True - a heart that loves without a clue.

For the first time the heart beats faster,
Just by a thought - you begin to foster.

A feeling very pure and intense,
That numbs every sense.
The world around fades, like a light of dawn.
And within, a new world is born.

Excitement mixed with nervousness,
A roller coaster ride of emotions that's seamless.

We don't fear, we just feel.
A new vibe that confuses, yet feels real.

The innocence that makes us believe it will last forever.
Fueled by dreams and trust, so light as feather.

As Life goes on, their bond fades away,
But their memories in heart choose to stay.

VAANI GOWDA

36. The Moon

It shines so bright,
And makes us forget all other light.

So divine to eyes, no words can suffice,
A glow so pure, it helps hearts endure.

A light that connects two souls,
Making them forget their worldly roles.

It's not just a celestial body,
But the mystery, hope and connection it embodies.

A poetic metaphor and a symbol of wonder.

A mission to explore, an endless night,
A dream that fills the heart with delight.

Every curve says a story,
Of form that transform, and of moments adorned in
glory.

The moon - a lovely tune,
that soothes the night, calming every sight.

VAANI GOWDA

37. The Women's Battle

A work-life balance is something for which she strives,
Amidst all the anxiety and mood swings she survives,
Until the pre menstrual syndrome that begins to rise,
And the post menopausal waves don't compromise.

She rises each time, with the fire within,
Carving strength from scars engraved on her skin.

She battles every struggle,
From emotional trauma to abuse,
Unrealistic societal standards to violence,
She is a resilience, wrapped in graceful silence,
And warrior in disguise.

VAANI GOWDA

38. A Message to My Girlies

Hey girl,
I know a lot goes on inside you,
It's ok to feel blue,
But make sure your mental health is never undervalued.

You may never have a clue,
A mental illness might be your foe,
Constraining from hopping around like a doe.

Seek help- it's not a crime,
but helps you climb,
even when pain feels subtle, even sublime.

VAANI GOWDA

39. The Poems

Most of us say we don't read poem,
That's what we believe and quitely affirm.

But infact we are surrounded by it,
In a song's lyrics, a meme, or a heartfelt text that hits.

A poem hits different, when it resonates true,
With the emotions that echo deep within you.

Poems offer a healing, by gently resealing,
The scattered thoughts that your heart has been
concealing.

VAANI GOWDA

40. String of Emotions

The voice we carry deep inside, and the expression,
The world may let slide,
The rise and fall in tune that guide each feeling we hold-
until we die.

We live for this- to feel and strive,
Each emotion that makes us truly alive.

VAANI GOWDA

41. The Rational Rescue from Limbic' s loop

Age of unawareness,
With a restless mind, yet filled with bareness.
It's just your limbic system on play,
Try using your pre-frontal cortex from today.

VAANI GOWDA

42. A Feeling that never returned

A love that comes once in lifetime,
Like a soulful music from wild chime.

You may meet someone more attractive or accomplished,
But the same warmth in voice vanished,
And the heartbeat once skipped is now diminished.

You don't feel the same magic and affection,
Because love is about connection, not perfection.

The laughter that felt lighter,
The conversation that grew brighter,
And the silence that offered solace, even better.

The souls aligned, and their presence that felt like home -
like bloodline.
A vibe that's not found again,
Reminds us some connections don't blend again.

You once felt something that's now irreplaceable,
A bond so rare, that's now unforgettable.

59

VAANI GOWDA

43. Beyond the Spotlight

Scientist, doctor or face on screen?
In chasing fame we've blurred what's seen.
What's wrong with this generation?
We've failed to honor the one who caused true
transformation.

The one who cures, the one who heals,
The one who brings the change in wheel of zeal.
The world celebrates the stars who shine,
While the unsung heroes walk on a quite line.

We worship status and glitter,
Often forget the soldiers, a true fighter.

Let's lift the hands of those who've built,
A better world, filled with true spirit.

VAANI GOWDA

44. Mother's Love- Above All

A love so pure, that one doesn't need to assure.
She gives her all, never checks if she's given less or more.

A love beyond words,
needs its own name to endure,
her care and nurture - Selfless, Gentle and Pure.

A foundation of whole family,
A glue that binds everyone so naturally.

Her sacrifices and tiring efforts goes unnoticed,
A person in disguise, like a true artist,
Composed and focused.

She gave you birth, even after knowing the consequences
it brings,
But she embraced it all, for she knows you are worth
everything.

She gave you birth, even after knowing it would affect
her health,
Because to her, your life was her greatest wealth.

A person one must prioritize,
A God's gift, worth more than any prize.
A love that never subsides,
It only grows stronger as time flies.

Her words are you power.
Teaches what's right and wrong,
Guiding your steps, making you strong.

VAANI GOWDA

45. Father's Love - Unnoticed

He never expresses his love through words,
Yet it roars and gently nurtures.

A pillar of home,
As efficient and sharp as Google chrome.

A quite king on an invisible throne,
Always watches you - A real life drone.

A slight change in his tone, can shake your zone,
Just one look and the lesson is known.

He like a shield,
Protects his heart, and keeps it sealed.
Yet stands by you, teaching what's right and wrong,
Guiding your steps, making you strong.

His love is hidden behind his responsibilities,

Masked by duties and abilities.
But in his eyes, you will always see,
The love and care that's as deep as sea.

VAANI GOWDA

46. A Green Flag Guy

A man who treats his girl with care,
With words and actions that are fair.
And in that love, the respect is earned,
For what he gives, he gets returned.

He not just hears, but understands,
He not just sees, but comprehends.

In right hands, you will always be valued.
With no need to chase or seek a breakthrough.

During disagreement,
he seeks resolution not dominance.
The warmth that stays with every glance,
Even in silence, there's a gentle romance,

Calm and composed, he holds his ground,
In his presence, peace is always found.
He knows communication is a key,
Expresses his emotions with honesty and maturity.

He doesn't flirt with girls around,
He stays bound to ethics, deep and profound.
He sets boundaries with other girls,
And doesn't make you feel dishonored or swirled.
A faith and trust that's rooted deep - grows,
Through his words and actions, that freely flow.

VAANI GOWDA

47. The Change

If a 20 year old version of me judged my thoughts today,
She might feel I've gone astray,
And if a 30 year old self looks back someday,
She might not agree with the choices I made today.
And that's how growth unfolds overtime,
Shaping your thoughts into something sublime.

People evolve based on their time, and the crime.
Let's not judge a person too soon,
We are all different phases of same tune.

One evolves with time and grace,
A glimpse of growth in every space.
The experiences that shape the core,
And quietly open another door and explore more.

VAANI GOWDA

48. Gratitude

We only see the ones above us,
And forget to thank what's already with us.

Value what you have, and don't just brag,
For the universe adds more to a grateful bag.

From a rag to a royal car,
Respect them both, no matter how far.
For each has its worth, at its own place,
Deserving of respect in every space.

VAANI GOWDA

49. The Weight of Words

Every word you say is heard and felt,
Don't just speak to talk it out.

Talk from heart, with empathy in mind,
Be thoughtful and kind.

Don't talk about health, before one with pain,
Don't boast your wealth, before one who have a little
gain,
Don't flaunt your looks, and make one feel stained.
Let every word spread kindness, and make the world a
better place to remain.

People remember each and every word that's said,
Let it create an art within and not leave them bled.

VAANI GOWDA

50. The Voice Within

You are exactly where you are meant to grow,
Let your heart release from the negativity that dims it's
glow.
It's ok if certain things go slow,
All you need in life is to gently bestow.
Every flower blooms at its own pace,
It's not a race, but how long it stays beautiful with grace,
with divinity at solace.

VAANI GOWDA

51. Love at First Sight

Something that happens in a speed of light..
Well, can love truly happen without any insight?
It's just infatuation, I believe..
Enchained by beauty, fame, and wealth .

For many it's their mother they hold near,
But I feel, the bond doesn't feel that near,
As it's something physiological than true connection that
psychological.

For many it's their baby they adore,
But that too feels like nothing more- As it's an
unbreakable bond of belonging.

Love can't happen at first sight,
Its the rooted trust, effort and respect that bears flowers

and fruits,
Not just the branches of tree.
It takes time to route a deep unexplainable connection.

VAANI GOWDA